THE UNDRESSED

JEMMA L. KING

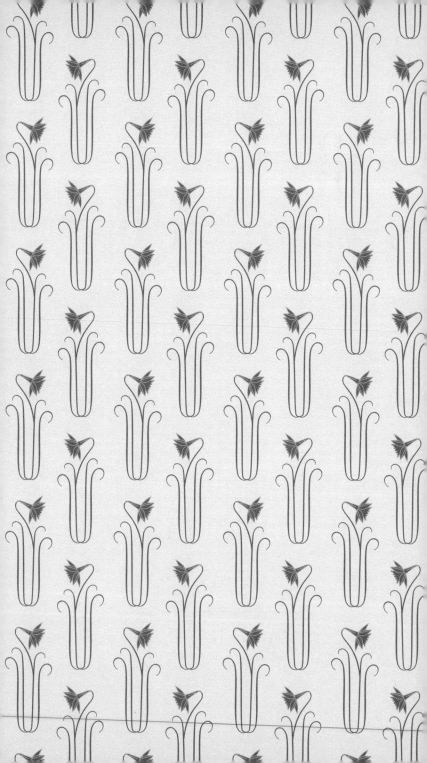

THE
UNDRESSED

JEMMA L. KING

PARTHIAN

Parthian
The Old Surgery
Napier Street
Cardigan
SA43 1ED
www.parthianbooks.com

First published in 2014
© Jemma L. King
All Rights Reserved

ISBN 978-1-909844-80-3

The publisher acknowledges the financial support
of the Welsh Books Council.

Jemma L King wishes to acknowledge the award of a
Writer's Bursary from Literature Wales for the purpose of
completing this collection

Edited by Alan Kellermann

Cover design and typesetting by Claire Houguez

Printed and bound by Gomer Press, Llandysul, Wales

British Library Cataloguing in Publication Data

A cataloguing record for this book is available from the
British Library.

For Richard Llwyd-Edwards

Contents

Montmartre, 1849......................................4

Laudine..7

Isabelle..10

Karolina...13

Aloïsia..16

Chantal...19

Léo Taxil..20

Elizabeth..23

Karla...27

Élodie...30

Sabine..33

Mary...35

Edith...38

Rebecca..41

Abigail..44

Dr. Knowlton and Dr. JC Barr.................46

Olive...49

Belle...52

Virginia..55

Lydia..58

Rosa...60

Sarah..63

Sheba...64

Ebonine...67

Eve...70

Celeste...73

Anna...75

The End..78

Acknowledgements.................................83

THE UNDRESSED

*When we define the photograph as a motionless image,
this does not mean only that the figures it represents do
not move; it means that they do not emerge, do not leave:
they are anesthetized and fastened down, like butterflies.*

Roland Barthes, *Camera Lucida*

Montmartre, 1849

Montmartre, 1849

A physical self found
itself fleshing out
in a Paris attic, slant
paned and dusted
decorated with Ottoman rugs,
tigress' skins, heads,
feathers.

A velvet shade just here, heavied with
the demand of grandeur.

The magician and his magic box,
golden-eyed Susse Frères.
He bends, beheaded.
Collisions in the halides as she
wills herself hoary.

Cellular, her
inflection outlines, unveils

as the slices of light,
a foot thick from windows
onto rooftops,

as the slices of light
illumine thin powder clouds
a universe of antique stars,
the membrane of empty space
shook loose

as she shivers, throws the stained
ecru silk from her shoulders,

as the smash and glitter
finds sepia form
on silver,

is sealed in glass
kissed with nitrogen.

Laudine

Laudine

I turn only to the night
where you live, my
Jovian God.

I am not a clean thing, I'll admit
to being an underling of the black hours
that fall soft as cotton sheets,
       your arms,
              your fingers,

they trickle in through
the pores of dawn.
My skin a conductor
to your Trojan comets, the
storm systems that oblate
my early hours, that cloud-band
the pelt of my love.

My love, do you exist
in minutes beyond the shroud
of crashing stars, the belt of moons, the
orange mess of
Jupiter?

I must wrench you free of myth – look,
here are my flowers, my
bridal sheath.

Meet me,

meet me in sleep.

Isabelle

Isabelle

Yesterday, I stood behind the counter in papa's inn,
the yeasty oak a-tang in the grey light. The opening door
dislodged the dust, a light show of skin cells danced,
and in this a man whose forty years had kissed
his countenance to laughter lines.

He lugged equipment of all peculiarity into the hall
before looking up. This foreign cat
had tommed into my alleyway,

my seaside-shelf last stop of a town. This inn,
a pension to those in need of the brackish
air or a briney menu to oil their drying joints. But this
I didn't see in his eyes. His paws pressed into the counter,
he smiled *a room, please*. I'd take him tea up, I said,
as he surveyed the perimeter of my hips.

*   *   *

In his room, plates and springs, polishing cloths
and bottles, boxes stamped *Heigl's of Frankfurt*,
the bed a workshop of mysteries.

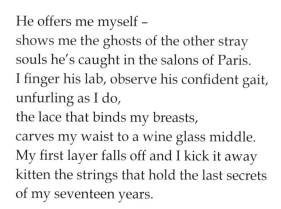

He offers me myself –
shows me the ghosts of the other stray
souls he's caught in the salons of Paris.
I finger his lab, observe his confident gait,
unfurling as I do,
the lace that binds my breasts,
carves my waist to a wine glass middle.
My first layer falls off and I kick it away
kitten the strings that hold the last secrets
of my seventeen years.

He orders me to stop, starts
assembling, his arm taut with effort
rubbing Russian-proof spirit
on mirrors. On the bed I thumb the
clean ends of my ties, waiting as he slides the metal in
and squints inwardly, a satisfied *aha*.

He throws pre-packed furs beneath my feet,
a spray of carnations on the table.

I giggle as he notices me for the first time in minutes.
Kisses my neck,

fills the gaps of me,
finds the queen of me
to catch.

Karolina

Karolina

Kotka's land gave nothing
but deformities.
The ice-packed soil so muscular and
heavily contracted
that tubers developed corners,
root systems gave up
their subterranean routes
and fattened in their thimble-small grots.
So when he found her – a sharp-faced peasant
with elastic limbs and
an unfathomable smallness, Dmitri reasoned
that the land had birthed her too.

Karolina, he would say,
come, get in this box. She was a wildcat for sure.

Did it with a special sort of Baltic
disinterest. Folded limbs in at cautious angles –
it all looked impossible, but then, measured, prepared,
she'd slip in like soaked soap, a box of boneless
human. She'd spring out, storm off.
But his thick blonde moustache
twitched at both sides
long after she'd slammed the door.

He saw the name of his latest exhibit
in thick Cyrillic, phosphorescent
stencils above the
Panoptikon, his
travelling menagerie
of faults and oddities.

He saw her furious Cleopatran
eyes centre-stage of their poster

Come See The Folding Girl Of Kotka!
The Nikitin Brothers' Newest Star!

And then, he thought,
he'd pluck the Eastern strings
of his balalaika in her cot,
bring her blood down, just one fraction

tell his story,
his provincial serfdom, lack of literacy and how
– clever as he was – he played the strong-man,
jumped horses, wrestled lions.

They'd travel Russia,
they'd live,
they'd die.

Aloïsia

Aloïsia

The last time, I came
to as the coldness surged like a weight
behind my eyes and the metallic trace
of my baby's blood gummed my thighs, strung, as they were
with purple strips of livery flesh.
Frau Marten's cooking pots and bowls
beside my bed were clouded
with a rage of reds.
Her hands swift, deliberate.

She twisted a rag, I remember it sprung burgundy
to the bucket below. She wound it
densely, pushed it within as I howled,
arch-backed as my womb shed the seams
of my daughter's beginnings.

* * *

He's asking me to look the casual nymph.

We stare out against the salted breeze,
its incense whipping my eyes to tears – each
follicle springing up to meet the advancing
wave foam and collapse.

This scheme of his, *popular in America*, he says.
*Walk towards the sea, that's it, cock
your hip that way, raise your heel, ever so.*
And I do as he says.

I look beyond to the khaki waves
exploding. Dissolving.

*   *   *

I was once a Catholic
but God has moved on now.
These hips have born bastards
from the seeds of a petty thief,
a man whose life is gin and guilt and vomit.
His fists erase the life he doesn't want
to admit that he lives.

*   *   *

If I could start again,
this seashore would be lipping my
children's impish feet. I would
chase them and reach
their goose-pimpled arms, feed them thick slices of brie,
the fattest of hams. I see them now, leaping
into the water's kinks and bevels,
shrieking their smiles
to a cold spring sun.

*   *   *

The khaki waves
exploding, dissolving.
I say their names into the salted breeze,
its incense whipping my eyes.

Chantal

I dreamt that I sent
calligraphy, dove-bound.
I want you, is all I said.

In the 1890s, Léo Taxil published a series of materials accusing the elite of France of practising Satanism. He collaborated with an eye-witness, Diana Vaughn, the alleged descendant of the Rosicrucian alchemist Thomas Vaughn. Diana related to Taxil that a demon had written prophecies upon her back with his tail, that another demon had appeared to her in the form of a crocodile and had entertained her by playing the piano. Taxil became a notorious celebrity and toured the country giving talks and selling his books.

Léo Taxil

Well first you must know the context,
this isn't madness, this is
maleficium behind closed doors.
Oh yes! The very best closed doors
in Paris.

It's this decadence! That fanatic, Boullon
in all his blasphemy, his black mass orgies,
the witch-cult of poisonings, infanticide,
forgery – an ulvose lusty trend if ever there was one.

Pan! Athena! Odin! Their false Gods, their carnal selves,
their nine-pointed symbols of Lucifer, oh yes

the Masonic Lodge on Rue Cadet?
I hear they strip girls naked, chain them, make them
dance on an upturned cross until the serpent himself
boots out of the fire, his ten feet of pan-animal
flesh indulged.

Unspeakable Communions!

They say judges and physicians masque up,
blade pentagrams on their chests – gorge
on girls and laudanum.

And the girls? Supplicant. Giving,
I hear, wedded to this pagan nexion,
this archetype of the base
and impulsive.

They give their own babes up
as promissory notes, suckle
the beast himself and
trace circles with limbs of the ash tree,
point at the stars with no shame,
turn horse hairs to snakes.

I'm telling you, Paris is
a waste-land now.
There's not enough Holy Water in France
to clean the stained winds of the
north, south, east and west – trice chanted into
and infected with his name,

Employ your rosary boy,
cast salt,
pray.

Elizabeth

Elizabeth

You thought me something
once.

On your arm we were
centripetal, a gold-
wash of angles, absorbent
as any galaxy
through a champagne flute.
Oh, how the world fell
to us in orbit,
how they gathered in their velvet and
crepe, their teal-eyed
feathers
drinking us.
My billet? My
inventory of blue
eyes, a pearl
décolletage and you,
you felt me your pet
love

for the night, as you
crushed the colour
of me into oak panelled walls.
That night as men
lounged in lounges wide-legged
and rum sunken,

as a horse high giggle struck the air and rose
as distant cutlery clanked in kitchen quarters under
fat stropped hands as
the music fingered
grooves in statesmen
hunched drunk and dancing, eyes closed.
The falling ribbons of opium smoke.

We ran through rooms
each its own chapter, a different story.
You chased me to the gardens,
the fountains upon us,
the cold sharp sober of
a viscous stone bed, water weeds threatening
my balance, my kohl
melting in the dark. The sudden heaviness
of silk.

Our rented moon blessed us
and only us, her ambassador
children, her poet darlings.

They hadn't invented the music
to match us then.
Our leaping challenge too anarchic
to contain in the iambic strings
that bent the soft June morning
that opened to us
two Piscean halves,

        completing.

The unwed scandal of us!
A lunar consecration
of bodies aligned. Drying
in the morning sun
as we slept.

On waking, we exchanged green blades
for rings. Later, my coach removed me, dropped
me in a place

you never visited.

This year, somebody else dents
your grassbound haunt.
                    Somebody else

plays the nymph,

but I was something to you.

Something, once.

Karla

Karla

You know Barnabus, I don't see
why I should own the disgrace,
when it is you whose body beasts and flinches
at the sight of it. Your odd
tensions.

So here I am, as naked as vodka,
owning (from the neck down)
a thing, a bag of blushes -
but that is all I am left with,
when alone and disrobed of custom.

My child body was the bud
that birthed the flower
and here I am, but
it's all hormones and politics
beyond me.

Why does my hand obscure myself in your presence?

You make me hate myself Barnabus,
because I infest you with lust, but
it's just a body, receptacle – vehicle –

Élodie

Élodie

for Rosie Myers

The noise developed
its own geography,
a sound web so low
that I swear
I could feel it
in the bones of my
thighs.

It was all incredibly irritating.

I wanted silence to throw
its soft auras around the
skin of my thoughts,
so I could fill it with her
dryad features, girlish giggle and skin
as soft as a mermaid's underbelly.

Sabine. That is what I wanted to think of.
Her Venusian grace, her stilled
gaze as hard to draw in the mind's eye
as the voice of the distant dead.

But no, a carnival
of chirping drums, a rash of accordion waves
breaking on my thoughts, drifting up from the
streets.
Moronic musicians!

Don't they know the subtleties of love?

Catching the photographer's eye
I re-arrange my face – Look! I am a child behaving!

But if you only knew
the softness of her lip, the intellect
of her touch...

I was less of a person,
more an ocean under the fingers of some sea goddess
throwing myself at the rock-face once
and once again.

Such miniature suicides
have nothing on the strongest of salts.

I must see her again.

Sabine

Sabine

I knew her sort. She entered
the bar, her furs and dimissive eyes
hiding a butterfly's curiosity
for my kind of flower.

We all marked it.

'Sabine', Lucille uttered in a tone
I knew portended mischief, *je te défie de la séduire*.

My success rate is quite something,
the challenge had me pinioned and
trained on her like a petrel.

I swam through the salon
and raised her pearls on one finger, inspected
them before seeking the red lip,
the clean eye.

In the time it took me to do this,
she was Sabine – broken and open
to my advances
which pushed her onto the street
into the alleyway
into my kiss.

PHRYNÈ

Mary

Mary

Throughout the 1860s and 1870s, prostitution became a serious topic of concern for Londoners as venereal diseases swept the capital at unprecedented levels. The Government's response was to implement the Contagious Diseases Act 1864. Prostitutes were arrested and subjected to involuntary 'treatments'. There was also a large scale campaign, in media, in sermons and within literary and visual art, to discourage women from a life of vice and to shame them into behaving in a 'moral' way.

Earlier,
I was chaunterin rand the Chapel
when I saw im Rothschilding is charms
at the girls. His whiskers
were curled in bacca-pipes an his gallies
ad a shine on em
not native to these quarters.

Oi Polly I says. *D'ya reckon he's got a bob or two?*
an she winked.

But every ladybird on the beat ad clocked him,
ad quit their puckering to push their
chests up and point their peepers
at is lordship.

I pushed my way through.
Alright Darlin, I says, *Lookin for*
Miss Laycock? I mean, why
mince me words, bent as I was on fleecin im,
Christening the watch that dandied up is pocket.

I led im past the other tails
whose eyes were all flashin a mean shade a green.
Went past Old Jacks, down the
damp alley where many-a-penny's bin earned.

Well! No longer ad I oisted up me skirts an
leaned into the wall
did a pack of a blue bottles come
burstin in on me business, grabs me wrists an
starts yellin that I'm one way
to the lump house!

They marched me straight to the slammer,
inspected me
wares for faults, gave me some nonsense
bout the sailors getting sick an how it's the
dollymops' fault.

Then, they locked me away, said
they'd straighten me out.
I'm up in front a the beak
In the mornin.

I'm 'opin he's one I've serviced.
I'm opin I served im well.

Edith

Edith

For Ari, Ifor, Susan, John and the Brown Family

I know that the oak that holds you
is oiled to the tide, is Jesus and crossed
to the hilt. Not men now

but seed-heads for a city, bearers
of flags and plagues,

prayers to save the heathens. But I see
those limed angel hands on
ramparts of squared slates

split from the earth by your father,
my father, maybe.
They say

Jones, buried in absentia, cholera, bound for Jamaica
Lewis, buried in absentia, typhus, bound for India
Evans, buried in absentia, consumption, bound for the East

And it has been one month since you sailed to St. Johns.
It's early for letters but I'll smooth
grooves in the stones, pacing.

The noise comes at night, when your voice is restored
to its northern shape. The salt of your skin, palpable, but

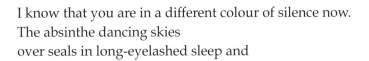

I know that you are in a different colour of silence now.
The absinthe dancing skies
over seals in long-eyelashed sleep and

icebergs rolling into the bay, morbid
scrapings on the sea floor. The ice floes kissing
like glockenspiel keys.

The depressed Atlantic shivers in that part of the world, shivers
and stops breathing. She embraces the fish, suspends them,
museums of themselves, whitened and wordlessly
drifting.

You may return buttery on whale flesh,
gilded on metals and skins.
Or emptied of yourself, the false gifts,

the blankets of the dead
handed over as flowers, bridges.
The guilt tripping you out of yourself

it's signature in the eyes of your children,
reminders of what you have done. Maybe.

And what of the landscapes lost to you?
The showy blue shoulders of icicles,
thick necklaces on cliffs that puncture
the stilled seas, the childless polar winds
journeying nowhere.

Rebecca

Rebecca

See, you look at me
and think me an anomaly of
what you know
of my century.

Dickens did that, fed you
a diet of upright citizens
and the earnest underclass –
the machine of London:
clerks' offices and good folk
with large families, struggling
to earn a crust.

But we had our swinging sixties
and naughty nineties a
full one hundred before yours.
Don't credit it, don't you think
that we slept under a blanket
of prurience, propriety.

Some of us showed our ankles.
Some of us showed a good deal more,
and profited, leisured and loose.

How many hat shops, shoe shops, purse shops
do you think were bought
by whores like me?

I went from knocking shop
to stocking shop
in six
short
years.

This, my friend, is London.

Abigail

Abigail

Last week, Sebastian and I met on the beach,
both conspiring against our better natures.
The shadows of the sun sculpted shallow waves
in the sand, pastel orange and pinked in
a summer evening's embrace. And here,
I let him have me.

I have lived myself into a corner.

I fear everything now.
In these moments, your invisible hands
frustrate me and my wedding band
blisters into my skin.

The impossibility of us
haunts me even as I sit tinselled
on this cool chair
for a portrait for my husband. Pills
tempt when
thoughts of you
thicken into something
nearly tangible,
but not quite.

Dr. Knowlton and
Dr. JC Barr

Dr. Knowlton and Dr. JC Barr

Our methods are imperfect
but we have learned
that the smallest quantity
of male fluid, admitted
to the female diluted in pints of water
is frankly,
a danger.

We therefore advise washes
of zinc and sulfate
(ignore the burning sensation dear).

Our custom is the trial and error of lotions.
women of the night must know
the use of acids - sponges dipped in vinegars (like so) or
wine prevents a mischief
of the immediate kind. Fasten it with string, admit it
(like so).

See the ease with which her
body accepts the device?
Well moistened in said solutions, risk is
entirely absolved, with no threat to satisfaction.

Now, studies have shown that withdrawal is not suitable.
It affects the male as would starvation,
the shock of *interruptus* leads
to intemperance, nervousness, an imbalanced mind.
These thin skinned French letters answer this.
They cover the male and block
the womb's compulsion
to conceive. Ignore the thick seam
down the side. It is entirely safe.

Nursing also prevents the occurrence
of a child. If the mother is already feeding,
the risk to you is nil. Spread this knowledge.

And what of the matter of disease?
This girl is healthy, look, but a redness here,
or a lesion there would necessitate
vegetable astringents.

The apothecary (for a shilling or less)
will supply you with a female syringe.
Fill it with infusions of pearl ash,
red rose leaves, salt water and the like.

We physicians take the front-line, try
to stem the tide of sickness, the abortions
that sully our city's good name.

Olive

Olive

Did you hear the immediacy of strings
sounding out my shock
in 12 frames per second?

Each cellulose strip frames
a short stretch of my muscles,
natural enough to me. Responses
to the director's command of
dramatic sadness Olive! That's it,
throw your arm up sweetie.
Yes that's lovely – hold!

I might lack naturalness,
my open mouthed expressions
emphatic and camp to a modern eye,
but I strive to show emotions
implied on thin scripts. My body
and face the instruments
that charm the audiences' eyes
from the anaemic sets, stages
cheaply dressed.

These are pupal days, and we
the black lipped embryos, our silver electrons colliding,
thrashing like the planets in creation. But one day,
when the reddened mouths of our kind
are seen to speak, are clothed in amethyst chiffon, cerulean
laces, hand loomed and split to the thigh.
When they walk the carpets and fill
news bulletins, magazines, idle gossip

you'll forget us forgers
of an artform: the silent screen!
The synchronicity of orchestra and muted gestures,
the pianist's fingers
tracing the ascent of arched
eyebrows, the coconut-shell
hooves of horses
the struck-metal shake
of thunder.

Our names will curl and spasm
in the liquid heat of the fires
that stole
our staged footprints, closing
curtains on performances that thrilled
the *fin-de-siècle*.

We are evasive as moonlight,
lost as virginity.

Belle

Belle

Oh what can ail thee? he implores,
American accent at the back of the studio.

Reminds me of his concept that I,
the fairy, am bewitching yet
solemn. Doomed to be the dagger
that some poor knave thrusts
himself upon. His fate
the fancy of some puckish pan
whose nymph-pet (*moi*), is the very thing you fear
when alone, in the woods.

This archetype, I wonder,
does she stalk the mists of a Bavarian forest, or
does she walk endless circles
around the catchment of a lake?

I would be horseback at all times.
Forlorn and collapsing
forwards with each
step the beast takes.

I'd be tragic, but handsome,
skin swan-white, and devastating.

I'd hope for Henri
who ignores me in the tavern.
I'd hope for his startled gaze

seeing me in my glorious true form.
My elfin beauty, my emerald
eyes marking me as Dürers Eve, fruited
and serpentine.

I'd mantis
him with a kiss,

bury him in the sedge
where no birds sing.

Virginia

Virginia

You wouldn't know it
from this shot but
I shrieked as I lay down,
as the first spray
stung my skin
under the noisy burble
and hiss
of an English waterfall.

It's cold, you see, in the Cotswolds.
The water stays ice-shot
even under the gaze of
a June afternoon begging
for a state of undress.

As I reclined, the wet grass
held me, each stem a stimulant
for the blood's course, the vital
components

alert to the gentle thrill,
of the world against my skin.

The sun, smoothing my eyelids
to the silky calm of an infant's
moth-soft cheek.

Sometimes, we wild-swim.

Those tentative steps

onto mossy rocks,
the giggles that give way

to the pulse of the river
turning the earth's sound
inside out,

roaring us deaf
to all but the thrum
of our instincts.

Lydia

Lydia

I am more netted than Arachne.
A funereal tease of
netting and lace.

I've got designs on hot-blooding you,
weaving you into me like
heavy scented bathwater. I am patchouli-smoke
setting a hex, pulling on cords that
bring your limbs to my level.

And men are weak. They throw their
bloodhound senses towards
the promise of horizontals,

but a woman suspending her myths?
Well, that's a time sensitive thing.
We moon creatures in our silks

can skin men in minutes
when certain vacancies noise themselves like
hungry children mewling,

that strip us in the shadows,
unfurl us
on Aphrodite's looms.

Rosa

Rosa

The corsets are coming off.
Do you hear that
murmured collective
of chant and voice –
a stadium at a distance
whispering now, but growing?
A riotous drum of cheer,
and if you strain,
you'll hear the snapping
of paper-chains that join
one decade
to the next.

The corsets are coming off,
those million layers
of restraints to hide us

bind us under the splintering
of our own ribs,
imprinting livers, jamming lungs

up – do you hear the brass now? Do you hear the
million sighs
of a million waists de-wasped
and the swinging of a million hips?

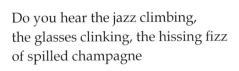

Do you hear the jazz climbing,
the glasses clinking, the hissing fizz
of spilled champagne

on Lalique split light – can you hear
the flowers withdrawing, the voices rising,
piano lids slamming, voices

Roaring, Roaring, Roaring.

Sarah

I am scarcely aware
of the arsenic stars, only
the mildewed smell of cellar.

Sheba

Sheba

I might look like a pharoahess
        but darling,
I'm much more exotic than that.

In my mash of pearls, venomous
cuffs and jade dragons of the Orient, I am Sheba.

The two syllables of my birth are
scribed in Hebrew, scored in the Koran,
taught in kabbalah. The mystical Christian
paintings arrested me, their less-than-flattering soft limbs,
medieval dwarf horses of odd proportions.

I became the hoof-footed she-devil, setting
a beat of beastly music
across Turkish marble.
My lions drew my chariot
over the sands of Arabia, I,
the caretaker of the wingèd covenant, I
the king-maker of Ethiopia.

I, Sheba of legend.

Yes, I foretold the cult of the cross
in the communion of hemispheres
crashing on Solomon's bed. Africa's horn

laying down a deal, the spice
and stone and gold of his son's crown,
a blood contract

to the King of Israel whose Empire's future
winking new in the sunlight, not yet
dusted under the bright blue eye
of modernity.

And I, I the synonym for
spoiled kittens in their jewels, queening falsely.

Malikat Saba, Malkat Sh'va, Nakuti, Makeda

Sheba.

Ebonine

Ebonine

I didn't really know what I was doing, gambolling around
and waving my dress like a flag signalling, I don't know,
the Isle of Woman? Confidence.
He asked me to dance and
clown for his contraption and

my nerves locked my smile on as
my undergarments loosed
and slipped down and
I was glad of it, for a second.

The foreign sense of my skin's direct
presence in the room fascinated even me, and as
my fabric betrayed me

my father crossed my mind.

All eyebrows and Godly disapproval. And then

the shot of awkwardness
remembering a body repulsing a father's
once-soft eye.

The bloody birthday that
stopped the love up, his
awareness of me sharpened
his animal rejections

and the condemnations of hair stylings
and mirror gazings, smeared lipsticks
and foolish rouge, those massive heels and my little feet.
Clip-clop, clip-clop
– once an amusement, a cute adult parody.

But those gestures corrupt me, enemy me.
I do not know what to do with these things
And the sudden stunning shame.

Eve

Eve

Ha! I *fleer* at the vanity of some.
My look is of the simplest regime,
because style must be uncluttered ladies!

All this pale skin needs is cold cream,
the depravity of sunlight and sometimes
the suction of auto-massage machines
that kiss at my skin like love-fish.

And the masseuse (seen each Tuesday)
pressures his fingers, winds tight circles
on my white waxed cheeks, oiled with the nutty
quag of almonds and petrolatum. The tissue food
fills out flatnesses you see, coaxes small cells to breed and
plump –
injections of enamels can be used but I prefer the facial harness
that straps the second chin, shoots the snow-marched
progress of bird's feet
across my temples.

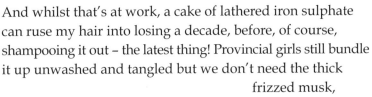

And whilst that's at work, a cake of lathered iron sulphate
can ruse my hair into losing a decade, before, of course,
shampooing it out – the latest thing! Provincial girls still bundle
it up unwashed and tangled but we don't need the thick
                                    frizzed musk,
we'll splash rose water, lavender, braid and curl our clean locks
to eight twists, soft pompadours bound with ribbons, barrettes.

And this waist didn't whittle itself, oh no, rubber corsets,
they cull the excess fats by means of heat, and we roll
around rooms to knock off the pounds, Quite a sight I'll say!

And then the claws, clipped, trimmed, shaped, bleached,
polished, coloured, rubbed with carmine, buttered to soften
the old paws girlish. And the (whisper it) hair? Needled
with follicle burning volts before the limbs, spread with
glycerine are pulled for coltish elegance, drowned in vichy,
tapped with hammers and busts bloomed under the hands
of medical men whose proven ointments swell us, bathe us,
tell us that thread veins and stretchmarks and birthmarks
can be bought away, absorbed like evil into hot stones.

It's all very simple. Quite.

Celeste

Celeste

When I think of him,
I think only of how I gasped
just as the love-smashed
moon bled into the clouds
more gaudy than even itself
as he held me by the river.

We watched the radial
midnight-rainbow:
a spectrum of oils
clashing and melting
into the star-sharp points
piercing cousin clouds.
I felt the trueness of something

and loved him. And now,
that is the only word I see in anything.

A tree, a painting, a dove?

Love.

Love.

Love.

Anna

Anna

Steel and brick casts dense shadows.

The city's floor lost light daily
as industrial roots, blood-fed, strengthened and limbed out.
An iron-shriek of sparks on tracks as more
fell into this pit by the million.

And I shot out of the shires
like a bullet from the barrel
of a gun

as the fields emptied and time aligned.
The Union Jack blackened as the hammer
of Empire slammed down, set
Britain drumming

tools and cogs. London, the ant's nest
in mourning, wreathed in fire.
Our hands warmed on the chalice
of import, export, war.

I had a baby, I had a mother.
I had work to do.

Above a gin-bar, my career began
under the hands of a sweating pig, expelled
from the Tartarus of workshops, whose purse
compelled my hips

to waltz his ecstasies out
on a horse-hair mattress more liced
than the mount it came from.

I did suffer once or twice at the rough rhythms
of men uglied by the open scowl
of the city's jaws. Their unwashed bodies
scarring the room with stale sweat.
A mousy musk.

This, until Katy
infantalised my hair, who painted me
female again.

Who presented me, a boxed doll
to a rota of better clientele

whose houses, wood and brick, cast dense shadows
over lawns and fountains, in shires
beyond the sharpened music of the city's
Satanic mills.

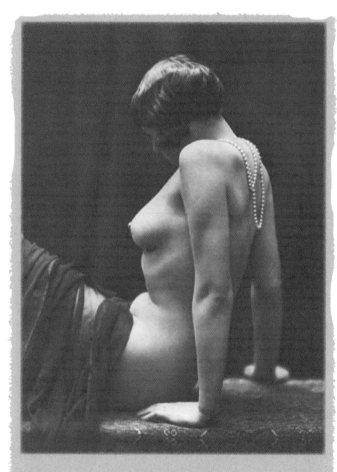

The End

The End

And then the world turned didn't it.

With every second that swam past, an invisible
river that grew, unmistakably,
to a sea, an ocean
with every second

her cells grew smaller, shrank their protean mass
until one day, as she combed her hair and saw
with every second that her skin looked thinner

and then there were children.
And then the children had children.
And one day the bells rang and she was at last framed,
contained, a masterpiece

of once-charged limbs, unclocked and sinking
inwards. Ashes to ashes

dust to dust.

And then the world turned didn't it.

Songs were still bellowed in the ale-houses, but they changed
as children threw off their playclothes,
played little emperors and baby-makers on
streets where ancestral atoms once

danced and fought and fucked.

And then somebody held the four corners of the globe,
pulled them taut
so that everybody slid,
tumbled shrieking into

a big, bloody mess in the middle
tangling horribly
on barbed wire and deformed
by a fast repetition of taps, each
hole punching
family trees back to the great sift
of the earth's fabric.

It's a long way, to Tipperary,
it's a long way to go.
It's a long way, to Tipperary,
to the sweetest girl I know.

And for the most part they were forgotten,
un-existed, their collective millenia
mulched and pulped, flattened

for their children's feet. Their children's children's feet.
And the world burst into colour,
grew capillaries and screens,
making everyone special, those billion
loveless pouty stares.

And then the world turned didn't it.

Goodbye Piccadilly,
farewell Leicester Square,
it's a long way to Tipperary,
but my heart's still there.

Acknowledgements

With thanks to the following: *Bare Fiction Magazine*, *Wales Arts Review*, the *Cheval* anthology 2013 and 2014, Dr. Richard Coopey of Aberystwyth University, The March Hare Festival Newfoundland, Literature Wales, Alan Kellerman, the V&A Museum London, Claire Houguez, Richard Lewis Davies and all the team at Parthian.